Genesis: The Creation of the World

Volume 1

Annie Hendren

ISBN 979-8-89130-986-9 (paperback)
ISBN 979-8-89243-080-7 (hardcover)
ISBN 979-8-89130-987-6 (digital)

Christian Faith Publishing
832 Park Avenue
Meadville, PA 16335
www.christianfaithpublishing.com

Printed in the United States of America

Dedication

To the Beautiful Children in our World!

Introduction

T his Book is about God Creating the World!

Natalie was going downstairs, and she saw Timmy and Alex. "Hey, guys, what are you doing?"

"We are finishing our homework," Timmy said.

"We are almost done," Alex said. "What are you doing, Natalie?"

"I have a play I am working on for school. If you guys get done with your homework, maybe you can help me."

The boys finished their homework. They quickly ran out of the house to find Natalie. They always have so much fun with her. They found Natalie in the gazebo in the backyard. Natalie had a sheet over the opening as if she were performing for a huge audience. There were two chairs set up in front of the entrance of the gazebo. Natalie peeked out and saw Timmy and Alex. "Please be seated," she said.

Genesis: The Creation of the World!

The boys took their seats. There was a sign hanging to the side that Natalie had made with construction paper and markers. It said, "Genesis: The Creation of the World."

"How can we help?" Alex asked.

"Well, will you guys be my audience? And please ask a lot of questions!"

The boys agreed.

Genesis: The Creation of the World!

Natalie pulled the sheet aside and walked to the front of the gazebo. "My part in the play will be God," Natalie said. Soft music started playing in the background, and she turned on the lights that lined the roof of the gazebo.

Genesis: The Creation of the World!

"The earth and the heavens were without form. What does that mean?" Alex asked.

"It means that there was just darkness," Natalie replied.

The Earth and the Heavens were without form!

"On the first day, everything was dark." Natalie waved her hands. "God created the heavens and the earth."

Timmy said, "Could you imagine having that much power to create the heavens and the earth?"

Alex said, "I want to be like God and have that much strength when I grow up!"

"We are so lucky to have such a beautiful world. God created it for all mankind," Natalie said.

Earth and the
Heavens!

Natalie continued, "Let there be light! God called 'light' day, and he called the 'darkness' night. This light is beautiful, Alex said."

"How did God come up with that? Light and darkness? God is so smart," Timmy said.

NIGHT
DAY
Light and Dark!
Day and Night!

Natalie then said, "There was 'evening' and 'morning' on the second day." Natalie stood to the side and pulled a rope and a picture of the sun started rising.

Alex said, "I love it when it is daytime!"

Natalie stood on the other side of the stage and pulled another rope, and the moon started to appear.

"Wow!" Timmy said.

Natalie then said, "I will separate the 'light' and the 'dark' and call it day and night!"

"God thought of everything. I don't know if I could do that," Timmy said.

"God thinks of everything for everyone," Natalie said.

"He is very busy," Alex said.

The Second Day!

Natalie then said, "Let there be water." She then pulled another rope, and a picture of the earth covered in water came down. "I will call this the seas."

Timmy said, "Imagine waving your hand and there is water."

Natalie then said, "Let there be dry land." Again, she pulled a rope, and it was a picture of the earth with water and land.

Alex said, "Wow! How do you create dry land? God created a masterpiece when he created Earth!"

"We live in such a beautiful world," Timmy said.

Water and Dry Land!

Natalie then said, "On the third day, let the Earth sprout vegetation, plants with seeds." Another rope was pulled, and a picture of plants appeared.

"Do you mean like tomatoes, peppers, and cucumbers?" Alex asked.

Natalie replied, "Yes, and a lot more."

Natalie then spoke her next line. Once again, Natalie pulled a rope, and a picture appeared with trees.

"Let there also be trees bearing fruit! Like apples, peaches, and mangos," Timmy asked.

Natalie replied, "Yes."

On the Third Day, plants and seeds were created. Trees bearing fruit were created!
20

Natalie said, "I am now going to create seasons." Another picture appeared with all the seasons. Natalie looked out at the boys. "Think about what happens in all the different seasons. In spring, we have the beautiful new growth of plants. Also, new babies from animals start to appear. Summer is warm, and all the growth continues. Things start to slow down in fall, and in winter, the growth ends, for a lot of vegetation and some animals hibernate."

"How was God able to think of all these details?" Timmy asked.

"I am now going to create stars," Natalie said. Natalie pulled another rope, and a picture of stars appeared.

"Stars are so beautiful," Timmy said.

"I agree," Alex said. "I love it when I go camping with my dad. The stars are so bright. It seems like you can touch them!"

God created four seasons, Spring, Summer, Fall, and Winter. He then created the Stars in heaven!

Natalie said, "On the fifth day, let the waters swarm with living creatures." Another rope was pulled with a picture of different fish swimming in the water.

"Think of all the living creatures in the water," Timmy said. "Whales, sharks, octopuses, and star fish."

"Snails, crabs, and lots of different kinds of fish," Alex added.

"Let there be winged birds!" Natalie said. Another picture appeared with different kinds of birds.

"One of my favorite birds is the barn owl. They are so cute!" Timmy said.

"I love the hummingbird. Their wings move so fast. You should watch them at a feeder," Alex said.

On the Fifth Day, let the waters swarm with living creatures. Let there be Birds!
24

Natalie then said, "Let there be living creatures!" A picture of cows, horses, sheep, and donkeys appeared.

"Many kinds of livestock. That is so amazing!" Alex said.

"Horses are so beautiful," Timmy said.

Natalie said, "Let there be beasts!" Once again, another picture came down. It had deer, lions, and bears on it.

Alex asked, "Would that be rhinoceros, hippos, and antelope?"

"All the animals you can think of," Natalie replied.

Natalie said, "Let there be creeping things." She pulled another rope, and another picture with ants, bugs, and worms appeared.

"All the creepy crawling things like snakes and lizards?" Alex asked.

"Yes, that is right," Natalie said.

Let there be
Livestock Animals,
Wild Beast, and
Creepy Crawling
Bugs and Snakes!

Natalie then said, "On the sixth day, let there be man!" Natalie pointed to another picture of a man. "God breathed life into the man."

"Hey, Timmy, we were created on the sixth day," Alex said.

The boys giggled.

Natalie looked out at the boys and said, "Man will have control over the fish in the water, the birds in the heavens, the beast on the land, the livestock on the land, and the creepy crawly things on the land, and he will also be able to work the land, harvest, and eat the food that grows. Man has the responsibility to maintain God's creations!"

The Sixth Day,
Man was created!

Natalie looked out at the boys and then said, "On the seventh day, let there be rest for God!"

"That is the day we go to church and praise the Lord for all He has created!" Timmy said.

"You are correct," Alex said.

"Thank you, Timmy and Alex, for your help!" Natalie said.

On the Seventh
Day, let there rest
for God!

God bless all the children in our world!

The end

About the Author

Annie Hendren has always held close to her soul that truth begets good and blossoms into light! Annie spent the first part of her life raising two talented, caring, and contributing children, along with many wonderful dogs and an amazing husband!